BIRTHDAY GIRLS

CELEBRATING
THE BONDS OF FRIENDSHIP

by Reeda Joseph

VIVA
EDITIONS

Published in the United States by Viva Editions, an imprint of Start Midnight, LLC, 375 Hudson Street, Twelfth Floor, New York, New York 10014.

Printed in China.
Cover and text design: Frank Wiedemann
All photography and text: Wright Card Co.
First Edition.
10 9 8 7 6 5 4 3 2 1

Hardcover ISBN: 978-1-63228-020-6
E-book ISBN: 978-1-63228-024-4

Library of Congress Cataloging-in-Publication Data is available.

Dear Friends,

On special occasions, what I look forward to most is celebrating with my nearest and dearest girlfriends. We've shared so many treasured memories—and they don't seem to mind when I forget to add another candle to their birthday cake! The time we spend together is the ideal opportunity for each of us to express how thankful we are to have each other in our lives.

Over the years, some of my dear friends have moved to different cities. And despite the miles, our friendships have not skipped a beat. A true friend is the greatest possession. I created this book and filled it cover to cover with sweet and sassy birthday wishes from vintage vixens. There's nobody better to toast to than our best girlfriends!

"There's nothing I would not do for those who are my friends, I have no notion of loving people by halves, it is not my nature."
—JANE AUSTEN

With love,
Reeda

With age
comes wisdom.
I'd rather be younger
and have a lot to learn!

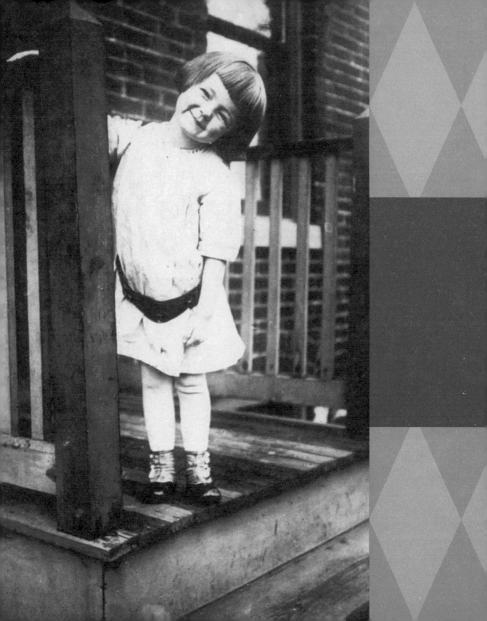

Just thinking about you makes me smile

What do you get the girl who has everything?

More!

Wishing you happy trails on your birthday and the year ahead

Old friends are so important...

that way
you're
always
the younger one!

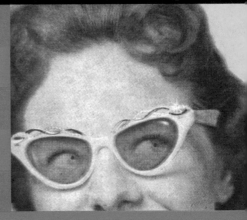

It's your time in the spotlight!

By now
we've learned...

sometimes
being a *bee-yotch*
is our only choice!

You can always be yourself around good friends

Honestly,

I don't expect a fabulous gift, a night out on the town, and to be treated like a queen on my birthday,

but it sure would be nice!

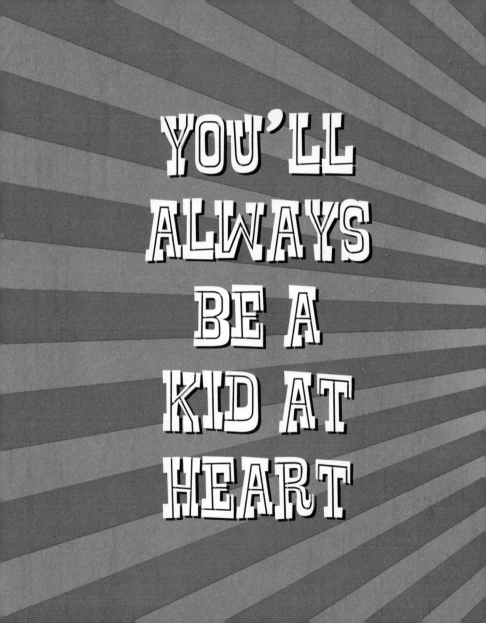

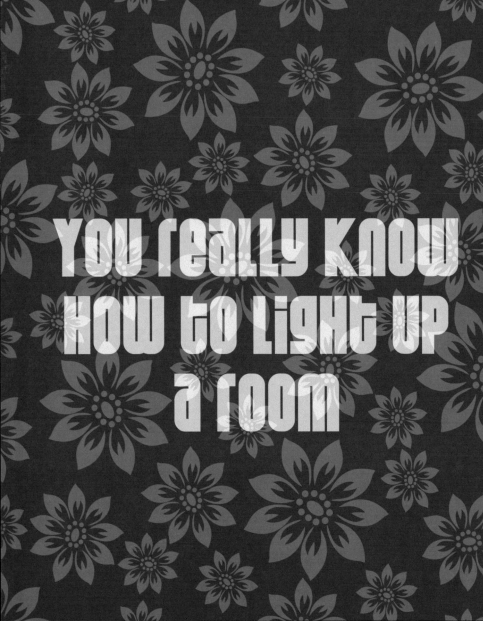

These are **not** the
Fifty Shades of Grey
I had in mind.

NOBODY WOULD EVER GUESS MY AGE... LET'S KEEP IT THAT WAY!

Happiness is...
time with gal pals

Girlfriends

make the world go 'round

hope your
birthday
brings out
the devil
in you

So many men,
 so little time!

Enjoy your birthday.

*Hope
all your
birthday wishes
come true,*

*especially the
naughty ones!*

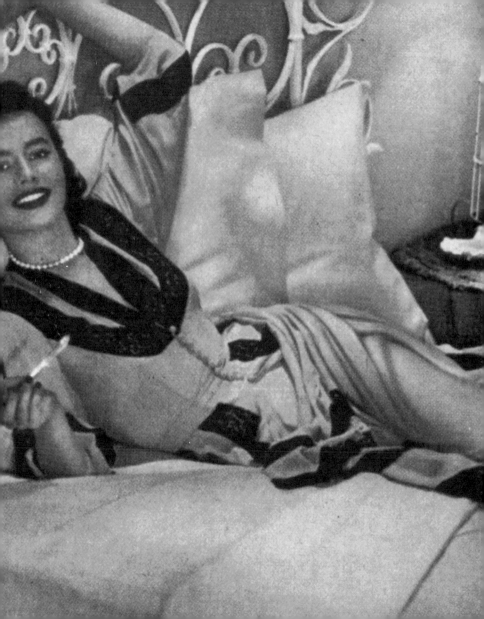

Enjoying our friendship every step of the way

Happy birthday, you wild thing

Birthdays are the
perfect time for
reflection.

Ah, the hell
with that...

let's go out for
margaritas!

Girlfriends are like our favorite accessories. They complete us.

Fashions
are always
changing
but our
friendship
will never
go out of style

There's a
drama queen
in all of us...

If the crown fits,
wear it!

LOOK OUT AHEAD!

BIRTHDAY GIRL

OMING THROUGH

Those days are long gone...

"Sweet"

"Innocent"

Birthdays should mean getting everything you want...

No different than any other day

Sometimes
a girl needs
a little attention

The only thing harder than
turning a year older
...is doing it sober!

About the Author

Reeda Joseph has been a collector of one-of-a-kind nostalgic items since childhood. From church basements to estate sales, to flea markets coast-to-coast, Reeda is constantly searching for (and finding) vintage images. A designer of cards and stationery for WrightCardCo.com, she lives in San Francisco, California.